KILLOCHRIES

Jim Carruth was born in 1963 in Johnstone and grew up on his family's farm near Kilbarchan. He has published two collections and nine chapbooks, starting with *Bovine Pastoral* (2004). In 2009 he was awarded a Robert Louis Stevenson Fellowship. His work continues to attract both praise and awards, winning the 2013 McLellan Poetry Prize and, in 2014, the Callum Macdonald Memorial Award. *Killochries*, originally published in 2015, was shortlisted for the Saltire Society Scottish Poetry Book of the Year, the Seamus Heaney Centre for Poetry Prize and the Fenton Aldeburgh Prize for first collection. His follow up, *Black Cart*, came out in 2017. Jim is the current poet laureate of Glasgow.

KILLOCHRIES

Jim Carruth

Polygon

This edition published in Great Britain in 2018 by
Polygon, an imprint of Birlinn Ltd

West Newington House
10 Newington Road
Edinburgh EH9 1QS

www.polygonbooks.co.uk

First published by Freight in 2015

ISBN 978 1 846974 62 5
eISBN 978 1 788851 62 6

British Library Cataloguing-in-Publication Data
A catalogue record for this book is available on
request from the British Library.

Typeset in Verdigris MVB by Polygon
Printed and bound by TJ International Ltd, Padstow

For my mother and father

Margaret Carruth (1938–2008)
Harvested love from all the seasons of life

Robert Carruth (1937–2013)
Cared for all who breathed upon the land

AUTUMN

In autumn
I come to the hill.

At the road's end
a rough track follows a contour,
climbs
        for a mile and a half
to a stop.

I clamber the tied gate;
bale string wraps this farm.

Hens search
for hidden treasures
in the midden;
shit speckles the yard.

On the barn roof
weathered rafters
peek out
between clumps of slates.

An old bath trough
catches water from a broken rone,
a rusted tractor beside it.

From the byre
a cow bellows,
chains rattle,
a collie barks.

I face the farmhouse –
its peeling whitewash,
boarded windows,
open door:

Killochries.

Reflections on a Shepherd

I. SCARECROW

I catch him first
on the skyline, facing away:

St Francis of the crows
in a skewed bunnet,

a misfitting winter jacket,
an old pair of dungarees

flapping around his frame
in the wind.

His outstretched arms
send a shadow

across a barley field
strangled by weeds.

From where I stand
he barely resembles a man.

Sae ye're the wandert yin
o oor Lizzie's bruid.

He looks me over –
a new ram
he might bid for
at some local market.

His scowl is fixed,
regretting the favour
for a second cousin.

He tuts and turns,
expects me
to come to heel.

Behind closed doors
he changes his mother,
gives her clean warm sheets,
props her up on a cushion
for my introduction.

She does not speak,
presents only a vacant look.
I offer less in return.

Pleasantries over, we eat in the kitchen
but not before a prayer of thanks
he delivers as I watch –

the mottled head slightly bowed,
wrinkles on his closed eyelids,
blistered lips,
his rough hands clasped.

On the table,
the steaming potatoes cooling;
a large helping of mince.

Three collies –
Glen, Cap, Meg –
seven hens,
two cows,
a calf,
his sick mother.

Tomorrow,
the flock.

II. PREACHER

And at night
he shows me
his one book:

a large family bible
thrown open
on the table.

He reads out verses
from Genesis 48:15
through to Revelation,

tells me shepherds
walked their flocks
across both testaments.

Meagre faith:
a man content
with one God.

St John 10:11

I am the good shepherd:
the good shepherd giveth his life
for the sheep.

To his
morning call

I mumble a reply,
stagger behind him
as he heads to the muir,
collies at his heels.

Out of breath   pause
look back at his farm
perched on the edge.
Far below,
the valley floor.

What welcome for me:
dark bog and gorse,
the itch of midge and tick,
the veering wind,
the threat of rain,
the question
Whit for are ye here?

Why am I here?
I don't answer.

It's my mother's doing,
a plea through tears

to get away from the city –
lies and excuses.

The final straw for her
that business with her savings.

Lik the collie dugs,
jist open yir lugs
an listen.

All day he teaches me
through the dank curtain
of his language.

A'v six hunner blackface yowes
tae be wintered oan this hill –
blackies bred tae be hardy.

Some words leak through
but offer little light.

On our return
Meg rises slow
from the back step,
goes to the old man.

Her grey-flecked muzzle
rubs against his leg.
He looks down and smiles.

He goes inside
to check on his mother.

The young collie comes closer,
snarls slavers through sharp teeth,
senses the outsider in me,
something not true.

I want to growl
my own anger back.

I retreat into the house,
sneak a peek at the drinks cabinet.

He has just the one bottle,
whisky a quarter full.
Not enough to do anything at all.

I surprise
   the evening fox,
my scent lost
to him
     in the wind.
He stares
        at me
     with amber
   eyes
and I
   at him,
a dirty red
dog fox, a hunger
shared.

The first week
I'm shown the chores:
feeding, bedding, mucking out.

My workmates:
barrow, pail, graip.

And at night:
table, pencil, diary.

The're an airt tae milkin a coo.

The black suckler cow in the stall,
the bucket, the three-legged stool.

Be shair tae let her ken yir there.

She bellows, restless, unsettled.
I follow and she flicks her tail.

Yir lik pairtners at the dancin.

I search for the secret code,
the rhythm to release the flow.

Squeeze them hard, they don't bite.

Long ages for a white drizzle
in the bottom of the pail.

A'll mebbe hae ma tea black the night.

For those first weeks, night sweats,
sheets changed every day.

It's clear my mother has told him
I'm *fasht* but not the details:

how I lost my licence,
my job, the flat,   Linda.

She never believed
it was only drink.

Tremmlin shivers lik a cowpit yowe,
a fever withoot the flu.

Ye wet an sweat the bed
worse than ma mither.

I wake to
ache of muscle and bone,
days too full of chores.
I never felt so rough
when I drank in the city.

Once a week,
sent down the hill
to the village
for food, papers, post,
I check the bus times.

On the lower slopes
beneath the farm, a small wood:
browns, russets, yellows.
Horse chestnuts, elms and the rest
catch now only the highest sun.

A single fir resistant to the change
points to the sky, defiant.
I could walk there, I suppose,
hide in its colours.

His old tractor can't cope
with slope and plough
so a neighbour works the only field
worth trusting with a harvest.

I watch him from the gate,
taken in by the symmetry.
I could be convinced
by the ease of transformation –

the turning over of the soil
burying the old failed crop –
but for the deepening of engine tone,
the dark smoke of struggle.

The phone sits silent,
disconnected the week I came.

If onybody wants me
they ken whaur A'll be.

He likes his radio
but has no TV.

The ootside warld
is hard enough tae listen tae.

Why wad A bring its troubles
intae ma livin room?

Looks straight at me.

St John 10:12

But he that is an hireling,
and not the shepherd,
whose own the sheep are not,
seeth the wolf coming,
and leaveth the sheep,
and fleeth: and the wolf catcheth them,
and scattereth the sheep.

III. SALESMAN

I watch him stand by the ring.

An auctioneer pleas
for the price to rise
but there's no response
from the crowd.

He does not want pity,
simply what's due.

His eyes betray him just once:
a glance upwards,
a prayer unanswered,

the gavel
brought down hard.

The future of the flock
rests with one ram.

Red medallion man,
his ram raddle and swagger
marking fast his flock.

After a busy week
we bring him in,
remove his marker.

Was it fancy wurds
or philosophy
that helpt ye
kep that yin
intae the fank?

I will not be drawn
to his debate.

For weeks so much rain
my socks rot through.

My skin so thin,
my face cracked.
Weathering too on the inside

through long nights
of sparking sticks and stag roar,

the fire caught in a single malt
he cradles for hours
but never sips.

God, he must know
what he is doing to me.

Let
my
words
tumble
off
the
muir
as
melt
water

to
be
shot
from
the
linn

free-
falling.

Fox, your dark back arched
    to pounce on sound;

    forepaws pin your prey,
fill your mouth with vole.

IV. CARER

His own mother,
who no longer
knows him,
cries out
Faither – help me
in a child's voice
from a bed
too big.

He kneels
in the next room
to look
into the eyes
of his old collie,
finds pain
in thickening mist.

He'll talk
one last time
to an old friend –
arthritic and lame,
lying by the fire –
scratch her head,
clap her worn coat,
wrap her in
a favourite blanket,

lift her up –
no heavier than
a pair of his old boots –
carry her out
beyond the barn.

A pause
in talking:

a wind
stiffening;
a shiver,
a shrug;

a glance
to the north;
a nod,
a thought:

a change
in the weather.

WINTER

Bone-chill morning –
hard clod and fog,

short breaths
of thin air.

I struggle up the hill
to feed the sheep.

No shelter here:
sheep huddle in hollows;

everything exposed,
shaped by the wind –

curved trunks of the few trees,
the old man's bent spine.

Sleet turns to hail,
raw lips bleed.

During these long sober nights
I attack his precious book,
take on his fallacy of Eden
with Darwin and dinosaurs.

I ridicule Noah and his animal pairs,
Moses and the Red Sea crossing,
the miracle of loaves and fishes,
picking away at his foundations of faith
like crows at a sheep carcass.

He does not argue
or give me a goad to kick against.
In silence he holds firm to his faith,
looks at me with a pity that hurts.

This morning
first snow on the hill

has a false innocence.
Valley, hillside, muir are one.

But death lies out there
for us to find.

The morning is set aside
for long sticks and lost sheep,

finding and feeding the living,
recovering the dead.

By afternoon, snow slips off
the small wood's highest branches.

The dark pine punctures through,
points to a hooded crow circling above.

For days, snow pockets have hung on.
I want everything revealed.
A mountain hare twitches free
and is hidden again.

Feet and fingers are lost to me too,
numbed by the day.
Only at night by the fire
do they return, sharp pin pricks.

It's feeding time.
While he cajoles the sick calf
to take milk from a pail,
I spoon-feed
a plate of tepid mash
to his mother.

Ye must be Lachlan's son.
She thinks I'm a neighbour
from her youth.
I have long given up
trying to correct her.

She and I caught in time
in the semi-dark
flicker of an old bulb.

V. LANDSMAN

His sparse words.
His silence.

His breath
spat through gaps

in a barn
of broken bales.

His ploughed neck
sprouting stubble,

thin soil furrowing
his forehead,

frail wisps of hair:
hoar frost

clinging to
granite's crag.

What future here

in an old man,
his blind mother,
this run-down barn,
barren earth,
a biting wind,
these bleating bags
of bones?

And he tells me
that since I've come
his prayers
are twice as long.

The day almost like
any other.
And at night:
no turkey
but an old hen;
no crackers,
no tinsel,
no tree;
no passing on
of small presents.
His mother asleep;
a tension
between us.
Nativity
recounted
from his
big book –
shepherds
from the hill
celebrating
the new birth.
This is not
my first Christmas
bearing conflicts
as gifts.

Fox, I've almost lost sight of you:
your presence is musk,
  a severed feather,
   a hedgehog skin,
    a twisted dropping,
      paw prints on snow.

We stay up
until Auld Lang Syne
crackles on the radio.

He offers me a whisky.
I accept just the one,
pass his test,
though he throws me
with his toast:

This year may yir wurds come
lik new shoots in the spring.

I walk outside –
so quiet here,
especially at night.

Too quiet:
you can hear yourself think.
Tonight the sky is full of stars,
a couple fallen
in the valley below.

This fleece
of winter
on the hill:

neither
cloud spill
nor snow

but dirt,
matted tug
and thorn.

In the last light of day
I catch the profile
of a single stag
on the brow of a hill.

He has not won
this season's fight for family –
that need to belong.

Hefting, I am told,
is the learnt behaviour
of generations.

Each sheep, knowing
the tracks and trails
of its territory,

will not wander far
from its homeland
across the open moor.

Who can I learn from?
I'm already lost.

Today I lash out
at the calf in the pen
who butts the pail,
spills its mother's milk.

*Don't you know
what's good for you?*

VI. STORYTELLER

The old man talks in code:
fables and parables

biblical and otherwise.
Tonight it's a dairy heifer

who wouldn't accept
her place in the byre

but roared a protest
from her stall,

kicked out
at the clusters,

flicked her tail
in the dairyman's face.
She'd give up her milk
to no one.

He leaves it there, tells me
the ending is not yet written.

I've had it.
Old man, open your eyes,
look around you – can't you see
this is not a success?

Tell me who has a wasted life.
On what basis do you judge me
from the heights of this hill?

I am sick of your prayers.
What are you thanking God for:

this year's ruined barley,
your bank manager's letters,
your dying mother,
your poverty?

Silence in that byre:
the old man's brief glance to me
an hour-long sermon.

At night I'm at him again.

Is silence not always
the church's answer?
Secrecy, collusion, cover-up

turning its back
on the vulnerable and weak
time and time again.

I've said too much;
this was never about the church.

He answers at last:

Better tae hae belief in ane hersh god
than tae hae lost faith wi many.

Morning comes.
Hen house silent,
     limp bodies,
a feathered shroud.

Why kill so many, fox,
when you can carry
     only one?

After months here
the hill has worn away
my few words.

My voice has let me down,
my hands are not mine.

A clumsy struggle
with an alien pencil that lies uneasy
on the hard skin.

I snap it like a stick,
cast the diary in the bin.

We try to ready the farm.

Up and down
the ladders
all afternoon,
hammering down
loose slates
with six-inch nails,
tethering
corrugated sheets
with bale string.

At night, outside
whistle, crash and shatter.

Inside, I breathe in
creak and strain.

Morning picks its way through the debris –
slates, guttering, sheets, broken glass.

A couple of trees have fallen
in the small wood,
the lone pine has lost its tip.

I turn my back on the farm,
take my anger up the hill.

Alone on this unforgiving muir
I rage at the old shepherd,
curse his King James Bible,
kick out at his blind faith,
wrestle with his god

        and fall.

St John 10:13

The hireling fleeth,
because he is an hireling,
and careth not for the sheep.

He tells me a week later
he'd followed me,

watched me break down
in the field of whins,

cry for hours
on the hill –
all that outpouring

that understanding
of wasted years.

Ahint yir een-glint
a sma hairt sair skint.

For the death of others
this one waits on gate-posts

or scars
the sky above, soaring

slow wide circles
hung high on crucifix wings.

Hawk eyes
scour the silence

for a faintly stirring
heartbeat ball of fur

stranded soft-pawed
in open ground.

Rush of buzzard thrust:
blackthorn claw

and curved beak
cracks gravity

through boned flesh,
eclipses day.

The end comes quick.

After a week
of bedside prayers
his mother dies

and I cry

      though I hardly knew her.

I try to tell him
that prayers
aren't always enough.

They ar
There's aye someone listenin.

The night after the funeral
his quiet words fall like snow.
Anecdotes, old neighbours,
a litany of names:
Lawson, Baxter, Wilson.

He talks of the old homeland.
He's stayed put
but the others left
by car or simple coffin.

He'll be the last to farm here.

With the end the beginning
of conversation:

Yir mither's a guid wummin.

Yes she is.

A'm sorry I didnae mak yir faither's funeral.

Neither did I.

Weel we cannae chat aw day;
we've a heap o wirk tae be done.

Our waking hours together.

Days on the hill,
the early signs of new growth,
the greening
travelling up from the valley floor,
the ewes filling out.

Nights are bible-reading,
notes and verses,
diary reclaimed from the bin,
quiet conversations,
a radio's distant wars.

Love song
of fox

sung across
    my night:

eerie scream
        of vixen,

triple bark
of dog.

By dawn
you're a pair.

    She leads
across the muir.

Straight-tailed,
you follow.

After a couple of weeks
a small fire is lit.

Her old clothes –
the nightdresses and baggy jumpers
I only ever saw her in;
skirts, shoes from her wardrobe
from before
the bed was her life;
the rotten mattress.

We watch
until the embers die.

That's enough fir today.
The morn
we bring the flock
aff the muir.

I linger

take it all in.

It will soon be
lambing time.

We set off
in the dark
to gather in
the scattered flock,

drive them down
to the in-bye land.

I want to find
them all,

bring each blackie
safe home.

SPRING

Put on yesterday's dirt;
clap the collie.

Check the cows
as swallows swoop.

Start the old tractor,
call on the flock,

join the chorus,
hoist the morning sun.

The hard-wearing
survive the winter:

half my clothes
remain,

one pair
of good boots.

The long walk
for cigarettes

discarded
then forgotten.

VII. FLOCK MASTER

He whistles on Meg,
calls *Away bye*,
sends her up the hill,

signals a wide arc
to gather up
his treasured flock,

bring them back
to the waiting pens:

shouts commands
sleeping sound
in his chair.

Patience is built wi the wait.
And that is what we have done,
watching the flock these last few days,
eager for the first birth
to kick-start the rest,

laughing at two brown hares
solitary all winter
on their hind legs,
throwing punches.

Happens without fanfare,
one slipping out unnoticed,
soon joined by a twin,
sticky and weak,
both testing their voices,
calling their mother,
who licks them clean with her tongue,
brings them to their feet and feeds them.

And we who are not needed this time
keep our distance.

Full-bellied blackfaces
                 and patient crows
side by side, sprinkling the hill with snow and ash,
turning their heads to a lamb's cry.

Anxious ewe waddle
                 and cocky caw-caw walk
follow the new-born's fragile steps.

Three weeks: one field
a deluge

of births and deaths.

We work in tandem days and nights,
walking a shepherd's trance,
straining to keep the lambs alive.

Frae their first braith
they ar tryin fir their hinmaist.

He gives me a lamb to save;
advice, bottle, rubber teat.

Drip drip of milk, long hours
into the tiny mouth, motherless,
blanket-wrapped by the stove door.

This bleating life-bundle
has to survive –

for the old man, for itself,
for me.

St John 10:14

I am the good shepherd
and know my sheep,
and am known of mine.

I read his bible at night;
it is the only book.

He watches me
but says nothing.

He does not know
I am taken
by the New Testament.

Easter morning: fluttering upwards
from a nest of moss
through hawthorn,
a flash of chaffinch.

I am thirsty for new language,
found oasis
on my tongue:
gimmer, tup and hog.

VIII. TEACHER

He teaches me

the living hill, the signs
of growth and birth,

the pacing of the ewe
close to its time,

the hoarse bark of colic
in a lamb,

blooms of wild flowers,
shapes of leaves,

the taste of grasses,
the pitch of finches,

the warning smells
of foot-rot and scour.

Today's lesson lies out in the field –
an old sheep with a purple red protrusion:
vaginal prolapse, easy to diagnose,
much trickier to fix, he tells me.

So we work together – I hold the ewe fast
while he starts a gentle easing in.
She continues to push it back out
so I am sent for some baler twine.

He ties some twine together,
pulls it across her shoulders,
runs the ends under her hind legs,
alongside her tail, up her spine,
across her shoulders again,
tight enough to keep her back arched
so she can't push.

If she pops it oot afore she lambs
it'll be yir turn tae put it back in.

By its hind legs
I swing the lamb,
clearing mucus
from its throat.

It chokes
into new life.

The shepherd slices
the skin of a dead lamb

to clothe the orphan,
to convince the mother
to give up her milk's blessing.

Ilka bairn needs a mither,
ilka mither needs a bairn.

The weather closes in again:
multitude of migrations,
urgent flutter and shuttle,
mud and straw,
feather and twig,
swallow's spittle cementing quick
a nest for speckled eggs.

I gather up in my pockets
reeds, feathers and twigs,
build a nest of pine cones,
find a misplaced memory.

Aye ye wir here aince
when ye wir very sma

but yir dad hit yi fir pretendin
to be a bird feedin its young.
A wouldnae hae him back.

Fox,
    walk with me
this night
among these hills:

chase the stars away,
    circle the wood,
find the scent,
track the prey I crave.

Days of May fruit,
camouflage of bracken,
cackle and wing beat,
chattering explosion.

Flight disturbing thought
or the quest for thought
or was the grouse itself
the thought?

This flowering language
fills me –

heather a blaze of colour to the muir,
I reach out to touch and name:

sphagnum, bog asphodel,
thistle, bog myrtle, whin,

cocksfoot, cottongrass,
devil's-bit scabious,
cowberry, cloudberry, broom.

Pockets bulging
with scribbled verse.

In this air, my writing
a flourishing of lichen.

I have eyes. I have ears.

At night
swapping verses by the fire:
my notebook, his bible;

questioning each other
on the intricacies
of poetry and faith.

Competitions –
presenting our own verses
in rhyme:

Spinsters of Hardridge farm

Sisters grim,
gorse and thistle,

grit schist kin,
shilpit gristle.

Neebours

Twa hardy quines
wi fairmers haunds

gied thir hail lives
to thir faither's laund.

Strang faith haes the maucht o saumon
tae bend an buck agin the currents,
leap the linn sure in the belief
o somethin unseen – the hecht
o the final spawnin grunds.

Even for him demons visit at night.
I hear him through the thick walls
turning in his bed, rattling its frame,
screaming at some unnamed terror,
calling on his god for the dawn.

Still more to learn
about lambs –

this education
of health and disease:

why lambs
should be wormed
at weaning;

the importance
of tail-length
and flystrike;

the reason
he'll never dock
a blackie;

the benefits
of castration.

IX. POET

Today I lecture him
on sonnet construction,

compare it to the dyke
we are building back up.

As he seeks out
that elusive right stone

I talk of fit and position,
metre and line-length.

He points to the hole
left at ground level.

*It's the weygate spaces
that lat in the life.*

Fox, I spot you
in the far field
leading your squabble
of well-fed cubs.

I picture your den:
small hole to the world,
snuggle of fur on fur,
the warmth of family.

Eight months late,
I respond to the first
of my mother's letters
and then the rest.

He leaves early for the village,
tells me I'm in charge

then spends the day sorting out
his mother's will,
a meeting at the bank.

He returns home late,
still in his uncomfortable suit,

his trousers muddied from a visit
to the small village graveyard.
Jist visitin auld pals.

He checks the cows
and sits on the doorstep,
talking to his dogs for a while.

Our silence at the evening meal
is a new understanding.
Words when shared will have meaning.

Later he talks for the first time
about the way his mother was,
gathering in a clutch of anecdotes.

Memories I don't have of my father.

I ask him about his coming to faith.
This no rational decision
but a voice spoken to him on the hill:

Aye, it knockt me ower lik a bull charge.
God nivir stappit speakin tae me

but there wir times as a young man
I stappit list'nin tae him.

Spring-cleaning the barn,
we muck out the old cow pen:
the animals have been outside for weeks.

The old man struggles
to bend and lift the compact dung
through the heat of the afternoon,

taking a grateful breather
as I push the filled barrow
to tip up at the midden.

On my return I watch him
bent over in pain, coughing up phlegm,
then we start to work again.

It lay there for decades discarded by the dyke
at the bottom of the garden –
a broken clay pipe, which I pluck from a nook
and offer to him.

It was his father's,
a smoker from his teenage years.

He holds it close to his nose
as if he could smell his father's breath –

A wis nivir guid enough fir him –

and throws it away into the field.

X. HEALER

Mending a fence
on the in-bye land,

I hammer the steeple
hard against an old stab.

Tight wire snaps,
lashes back,

its ravel and grasp
wraps fast

my arm in blood,
traps me in rusted barbs.

He unwinds me
from the wire snare,

takes me back to the farm,
sits me at the table,

tends the wounds,
cleans my scarred hands,

dabs each cut with whisky,
scribes for me words that won't wait.

The collies come now
to my two-fingered whistle,
the hens stay on the nest
as I slip away warm eggs.
The calf sucks my thumb,
my palm on its mother's flank,

and after all this time
I walk to the small wood,
the one pine just part of the canopy
that shades my walk.

Senses colour the journey:
scent and touch, leaf and bark;
elm, ash and beech;
song of finch and thrush.

I can tell the individual
from the throng in each dawn chorus
and know it has a voice,
a place where it belongs.

SUMMER

Fox,
we're both
changing:
unkempt, impatient
scratching at old fur,
beneath this slow moult
of winter coat –
leaner and sleeker.

Clippers
and cable snake

my less than
certain progress

though there's pride
in the end

at the unpeeling
of each ewe

that jumps away
from its burden:

dipping
a baptism;

shearing
a resurrection.

They came in droves
wi their shears

frae the fairms
athort the law
tae gie us

a day's clippin
swapped later fir
anither clippin,

a darg at the hay,
a castin o peats,
a loan o the Clydesdale,

help keppin the stirks
or in the back end
a haund liftin tatties.

A day away;
a chance tae catch up;
a laugh, a smoke,
a fairmer's lunch.

St John 10:15

As the Father knoweth me,
even so know I the Father:
and I lay down my life
for the sheep.

His legs have been troubling him
more and more each month.
This afternoon despite the pain
he drops to his arthritic knees,
reaches into the stream
guddling among the rocks,
feeling the tug of green weed,
tickling darting shadows,
flips out onto the bank
a stippled arc of rainbow
that shimmers and glistens.
This offering at my feet –
his miracle,
this dripping gift of fish.

We spot her first –
a hen harrier
rising from
a nest of grass,

flying low
to whin cover,
rolling over
in mid air

to catch
in her talons
a small rabbit
dropped slow

from a partner
above her:
manna
of prey.

The first Saturday in July
a ram and three ewes
emerge from his battered pick-up
to the tents and rings of the local show.

We herd them into their pen,
curry-comb dirty wool, scrub muck
from their hard heads,
whiten with talc.

He demonstrates how to hold sheep,
show each off to its best,
then retires to the pick-up
as our ram comes first.

I'm left to wander between
pony-club tantrums,
splutter of vintage tractors,
flurry of drums, first wheeze of pipes.

Beer tent is a drunken bellow,
young farmers fall over
in the tug of war;
swear at majorettes.

An unintelligible PA system
announces the prize giving.
Somebody Somebody's wife
hands them out.

After cattle, the sheep cups.
He pushes me forward.
I pick up the trophy:
we share the moment.

It is a surprise to everyone
that he comes to the barn dance.

And I'm in the spotlight –
strangers' gazes, laughter,
beer, whisky, noise.

He watches me struggle
at the dancing, happy to watch.

We are both asked again and again
How is it on the hill
with that man?

This night on his return
he struggles with his boots.
I untie each lace for him.

Later, because you never know
where a journey will lead,
we arrive at discussions on love:

caring mothers, strict fathers,
God's complex love for us.
He tells me
Kirk an state hae failt faith.

I talk of girlfriends,
the beginnings, the many ends,
reunions and rows,
and it feels good to let it out.

When it's his turn he simply says
There wis somebody aince

and that is all
and that is everything.

There they are
when I'd almost stopped looking:
that rare glimpse from downwind
of the herd on the muir.

I stare at them for minutes,
hinds and their young
like the shadow of a small cloud
always moving, always alert.

I watch until they are gone,
unwilling to give up this moment.

XII. SINGER

Twice
I've caught him
singing
something other
than hymns.

Once when
he was fixing
the old tractor
he coupled
verse and chorus
for a light ballad,
a mother's gift
to her only son,
a hand-me-down,
a childhood
memory
I stopped short
with my cough.

The other time
I stayed silent
behind
the barn door
listening to
his low rumble
of vowels,
rocks caught
in a slow coarse-
throated river.

Tonight after
Hallowed be thy name
the Lord's prayer falters,
his voice brittle:
a blackbird fledgling.
Breathless, he wheezes
thy will be done,
then slightly behind,
a deeper echo
repeats his lines,
joins his struggle,
strengthens
his journey of words,
helps him reach
the *forever*
Amen.

St John 10:16

And other sheep I have,
which are not of this fold:
them also I must bring,
and they shall hear my voice;
and there shall be one fold,
and one shepherd.

Jist open yir lugs
an listen –

The old man's first advice.

In the wood, on the hill
and up onto the muir;

in the dawn and sunset,
the birdsong and the breeze.

I am listening.
Shape me, make me new.

Fox
panting
in the long grass.
Your coarse fur's
red and browns
catching the sun,
long muzzle,
erect ears,
echo of teeth
the work
of another.
In your bark
the song.

Through these seasons the old man is slowly going deaf:
another finch or warbler lost from his dawn chorus;
each bird taking turns to bow out until those left
can barely muster a hedgerow quartet,
shrinking quick to a duet of gulls,
a mocking black squawk
of crow.

Second chance arrives –
an old professor's letter

talks of potential,
offers a part-time post

beginning next semester.
I sit on the decision for a week.

I cannot tell the old man
but he knows now

how to read my silences
and that I must go.

The tremor
in his voice

could be for
an ailing ewe

or a collie
kept at the vets

or grief at the death
of a close friend

but today
it's the news

that Larkfield's
empty farmhouse

has been sold
for a country retreat:

Foriver lost,
foriver lost.

These last weeks –
making the most of long days.

The counting down
of tasks done together.

My words in a rush
to capture the old man and the hill.

But what use am I to him?
My poems cannot stretch a helping hand,

my words will never fill his run-down barn,
my lines cannot defend his fragile land.

All that I am left with is this:
his faith, his unshakable belief in prayer.

So I begin in faltering words
for have not all the words been said before

or is each new voice that calls your name
the sweetest song?

I hear his shout and start running,
find him out cold in the stall
under the feet of the big heifer,
who must have kicked him
on his way down.

I drag him away from the stall,
limp in my arm,
his face swollen, bloodied.

Old man, don't die on me.

She comes unannounced
into his bedroom,
this old woman in working clothes,

to tend his wounds,
her hands rough from farming,

prays at his bedside,
tears in her eyes,
willing him to wake.

This was the dream
I had for the old man
but it never happened.

When he wakes
it is only me he sees.

The doctor says
he was lucky:

he had gone to pare
the cow's lame foot
and ended up with

three broken ribs,
two teeth lost,
a cracked cheekbone,
legs covered in bruises,
face swollen,
eyes blackening.

He was lucky
I was there
or that would have been it.

For the first week
I feed him soup
the way I fed his mother,
read the bible to him,
pray with him,
listen to his laboured breaths
as he sleeps.

The next couple of weeks
he struggles with his clothes,
shuffles about the house.

Curse ma slow mend.

Too tired for the flock
he stays at home,
gives out commands,
hands me his crook.

Its hazel shank
has taken his weight
for years on the muir.

Its ram's horn handle,
cracked and worn,
can hook and kep
stubborn blackies.

Two elements
– forest and flock –
joined as one for him
to work the hill.

Their unusual pairing
a sharing of tasks;
a practical union
for all the seasons.

I steer my look between curled horns,
take time to seek out the difference
in every blackie's face,

their short hair stretched
skin-tight over hard skulls.

On the muzzle of a ram
I see the linn spray:

a milky way spread
across the night sky,

reaching up to his eyes –
orbiting planets
returning my gaze.

Back on his feet I find him
in the barley field
I've watched grow from seed.

He reaches out, rubs some heads
in his palm: *The hairst is ready*.

Two days later we hear the harvester
climb the road to the farm,
a tractor and trailer behind.

The few acres take little time.
With nowhere to store it,
the grain is taken away.

After the big machines leave
we are left to coax the old baler
into action along the rows.

I follow behind the tractor,
Stacking the bales
In the stubbled field till dusk.
A guid day fir the hairst.

That final desperate rush
to capture the hill:

I cannot lose this harvest,
I need to store it all.

Fox, this last week
though I seek you out
you hide from me.

The suckler cow, whose time it is,
bellows from the barn, and we go to her.

I slip bale strings over the front legs of the calf
and am ready to lead the task.
The old man sits down, throws me advice:

Don't pull agin her, wirk wi her
back nice an easy – relax when she does.

I lean back, in for the long haul.
No one seems to be in any rush.
Hours until the lolling tongue and head appear,

its shoulders too wide, so I twist
and turn till the calf frees itself,
slips out onto the straw in the first light,
stickiness licked off by its mother.

I wis worried for a while,
but he's a guid healthy son,
a real credit tae his mither.

I tell him faith
is in the seed,
the tree, the leaf

that falls away
too easy in
the cold breeze.

He asks
Is the kirk the tree,
ilka lost soul a leaf?

No, I reply.
The church today
is the fallen leaf;

those still clinging
to the branch
the real fruit.

Last supper:

the meal
tender,

hand-picked
from the flock

with a life
to be talked of,

a bloodline,
a history.

We celebrate
its seasons

and ours.

XIII. GUIDE

Pack up yir hairst o wurds.
May it feed the hunger in others.

There is no talk of return,
both too afraid of the future.

He hands me his mother's bible,
a parting gift:

Son, here, take this –
a pillow fir the hard grun.

Each arthritic finger unfurls from a fist
as he offers his hand to me

and I leave the hill
forever in your grip.

Killochries

His church
a field;

its windows
clouds passing.

Its congregation
slender elms

growing from
coarse grass;

its choir
starling and lark.

Its sermon
the seasons;

its gospel
gorse fire.

Its prayers
seed scattered

on an acre
for God.

GLOSSARY

ahint	*behind*
athort	*across, over*
bairn	*child*
blackies	*Blackface sheep*
braith	*breath*
bruid	*brood*
castin	*casting, cutting*
cowpit	*overturned, fallen*
darg	*a days work*
een-glint	*eye sparkle*
faither	*father*
fank	*sheep pen*
fasht	*troubled, bothered*
gimmer	*a two-year-old ewe*
graip	*large farming fork*
hairt	*heart*
hecht	*promise*
hersh	*harsh*
hinmaist	*last, furthest behind*
hog	*young sheep*
in-bye	*higher quality land nearer to the farm*
ilka	*every*

ken	*to know, be aware of, apprehend, learn a fact*
kep(pin)	*contain(ing), catch(ing)*
kirk	*church*
law	*rounded hill*
linn	*a waterfall, cascade of water*
lugs	*ears*
maucht	*might, bodily strength, power*
mither	*mother*
muir	*a moor, a heath, rough grazing*
quines	*young women*
rone	*roof gutter, drainpipe*
sair	*sorely, grievous, (of an ailment causing physical or mental pain or distress)*
saumon	*salmon*
shair	*sure*
shilpit	*emaciated*
skint	*skinned*
sma	*small*
stirk	*heifer*
tremmlin	*trembling*
tup	*an uncastrated male sheep*

wandert	*lost, led astray*
weygate	*a passageway,*
	thoroughfare, room,
	space
yin	*one*
yowes	*ewes*

ACKNOWLEDGEMENTS

I would like to thank all those who have helped this book travel a little further down the road, whether offering feedback or support. I am grateful to the Scottish Book Trust and in particularly Sarah Ream for ensuring the book reached its final destination.